BOOK 1

Current Hits for Teens

8 Graded Selections for Early Intermediate Pianists

Arranged by
Dan Coates

Teenage students love being able to play popular pieces by their favorite recording artists or from blockbuster movies and TV shows. This collection includes accessible arrangements of pop and movie hits from Maroon 5, The Hobbit, Katy Perry, Selena Gomez & the Scene and many more! The arrangements are "teacher friendly," while remaining faithful to the sound of the original recording. In this early-intermediate collection, 16th notes are avoided, and key signatures are limited to no more than two flats or sharps.

Produced by
Alfred Music
P.O. Box 10003
Van Nuys, CA 91410-0
alfred.com

D1275497

ISBN-10: 0-7390-9608-7
ISBN-13: 978-0-7390-9608-6

Cover Images
A piano keyboard waves on white: © shutterstock.com / Dr. Cloud •
stage with light and smoke background: © shutterstock.com / Filipe B. Varela

THE BIG BANG THEORY (MAIN TITLE)

Words and Music by ED ROBERTSON
Arranged by Dan Coates

DAYLIGHT

Words and Music by SAM MARTIN, MASON LEVY,
ADAM LEVINE and MAX MARTIN
Arranged by Dan Coates

Brightly

Lyrics (verse 1 / verse 2):

1. Here I am wait - ing,___ I'll have to leave soon.___ Why am I___ in my arms,___ so

2. Here I am star - ing___ at your per - fec - tion___ Why am I___ so

hold - ing on? We knew this day would come,___ we knew it all a - long.___

beau - ti - ful. The sky is get - ting light,___ the stars are burn - ing out.___

How did it come so fast?___ This is our___ last night,___

Some - bod - y slow it down.___ This is way___ too hard___

___ but it's late___ and I'm try - ing not___ to sleep.___

___ 'cause I know when the sun___ comes up I will leave.

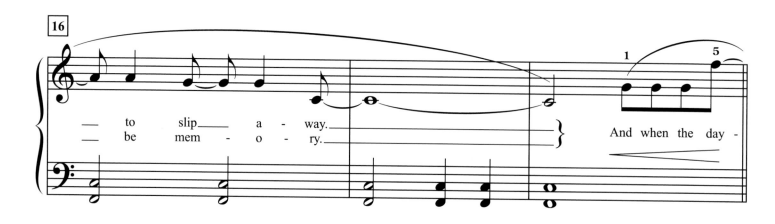

I need to hold you so close. Oh. Oh.

Oh. Oh.

Oh. Oh.

mf I nev-er want-ed to stop because I don't want to start

FIREWORK

Words and Music by KATY PERRY, MIKKEL ERIKSEN,
TOR ERIK HERMANSEN, SANDY WILHELM and ESTER DEAN
Arranged by Dan Coates

Moderately, with a steady beat

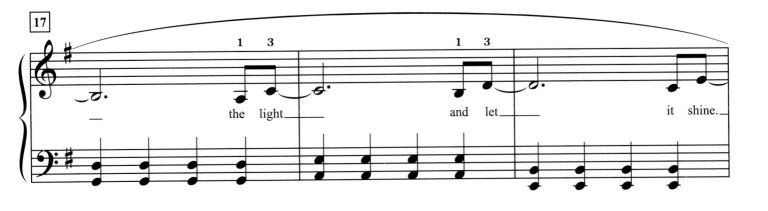

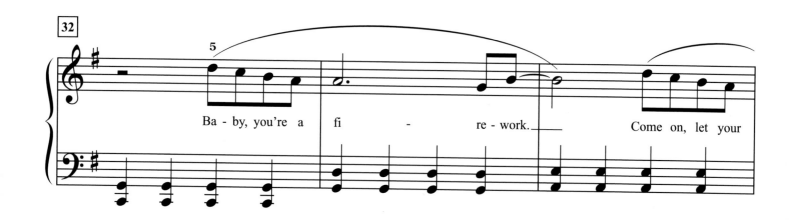

col - ors burst.___ Make 'em go___ "Ahh, ahh,___ ahh."

You're gon - na leave them all in awe, awe,___ awe.___

Boom, boom,___ boom, e - ven bright - er than the moon, moon,___ moon.___

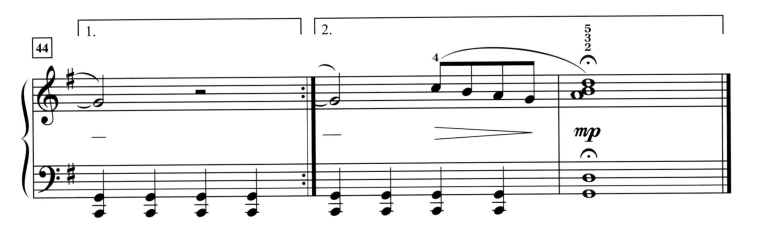

1.　　2.

GLAD YOU CAME

Words and Music by EDWARD DREWETT,
WAYNE HECTOR and STEVE MAC
Arranged by Dan Coates

else can see you and me. And turn the lights out now.__ Now I'll take you by the

hand,__ hand you an - oth - er drink.__ Drink it if you can.__ Can you spend a lit - tle

time?__ Time is slip - ping a - way, a - way from us so stay. Stay with me, I can

make, make you glad you came. The sun goes down, the stars come

out. And all that counts is here and now. My u - ni -

verse will nev - er be the same. I'm glad you came. I'm glad you

came.
mf

So glad you came. The sun goes down, the stars come out. And all that

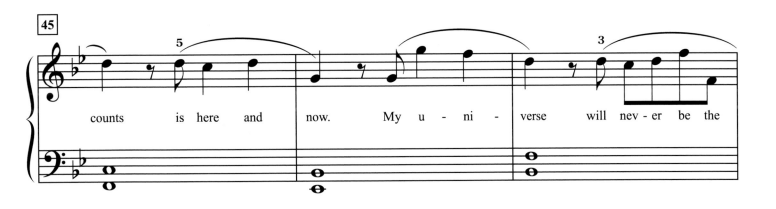

I'm glad you

counts is here and now. My u - ni - verse will nev - er be the

same. I'm glad you came. I'm glad you came.

LOVE YOU LIKE A LOVE SONG

Words and Music by ANTONINA ARMATO,
ADAM SCHMALHOLZ and TIM JAMES
Arranged by Dan Coates

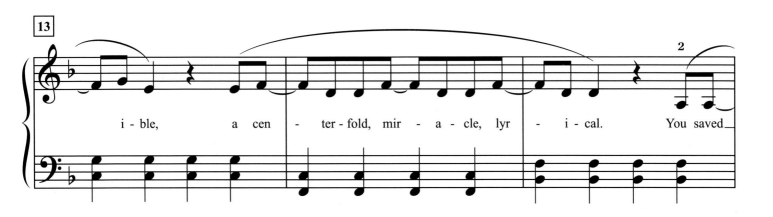

A VERY RESPECTABLE HOBBIT

(from *The Hobbit: An Unexpected Journey*)

Music by HOWARD SHORE
Arranged by Dan Coates

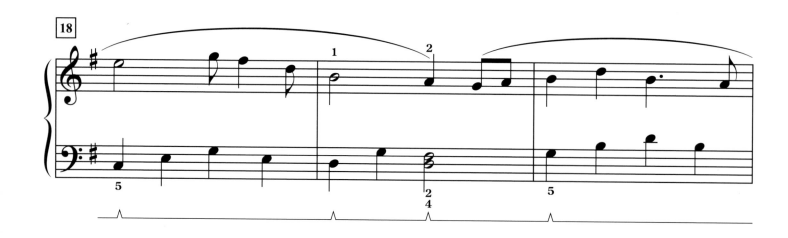

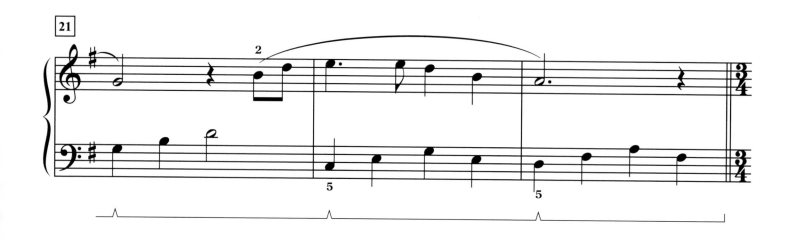

MISTY MOUNTAINS
(from *The Hobbit: An Unexpected Journey*)

Lyrics Adapted by FRAN WALSH and PHILIPPA BOYENS
Music by DAVID DONALDSON, DAVID LONG,
STEVE ROCHE and JANET RODDICK
Arranged by Dan Coates

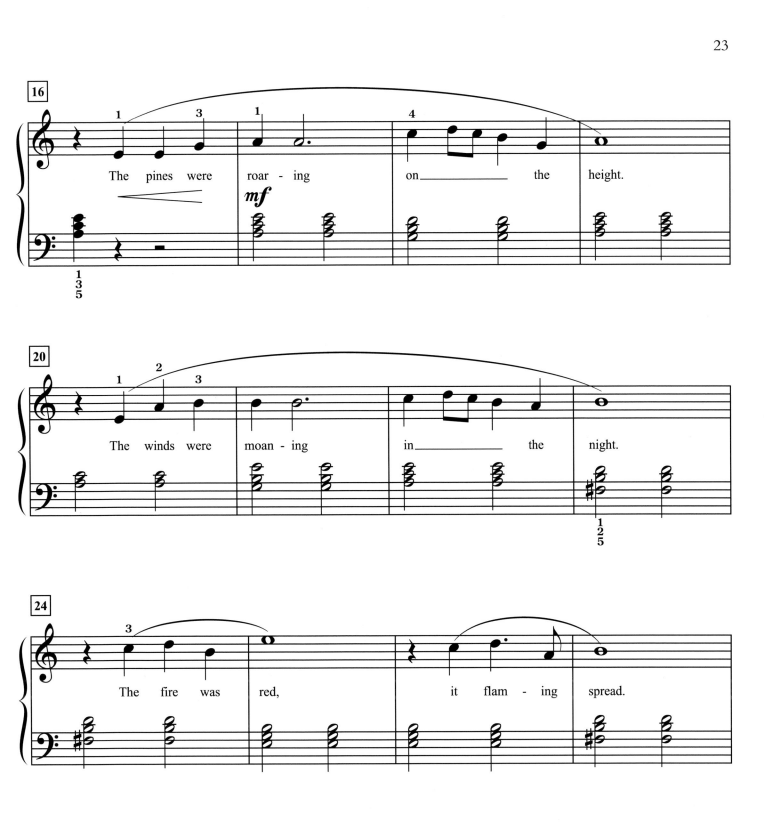

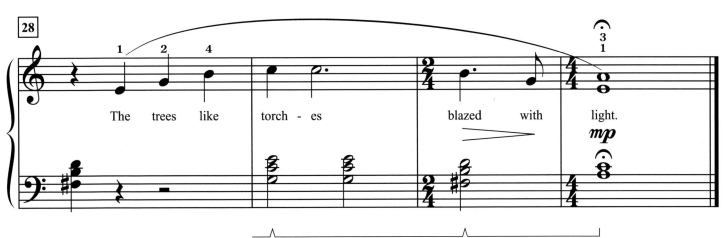

SOME NIGHTS

Words and Music by NATE RUESS, JEFF BHASKER,
ANDREW DOST and JACK ANTONOFF
Arranged by Dan Coates

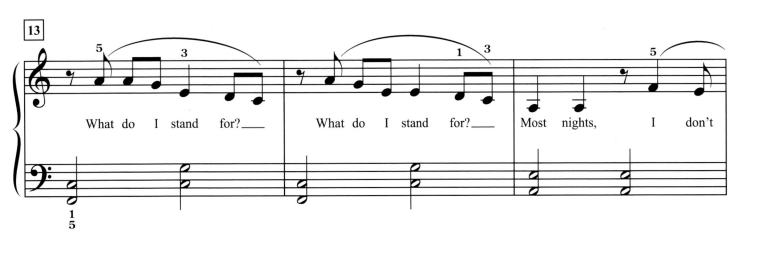

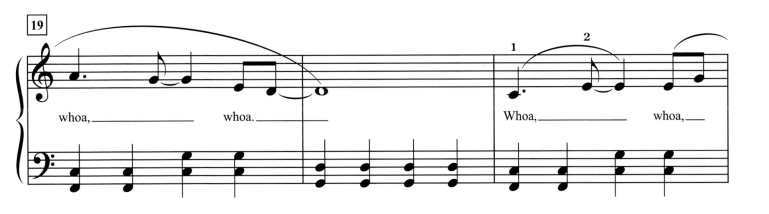

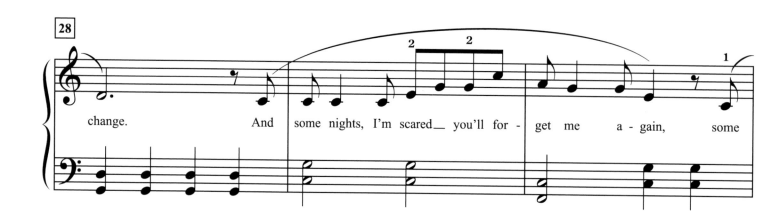

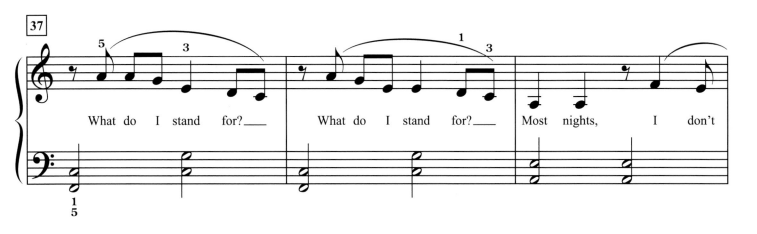